Without Music

Poems

By Winnie Akousika DOGBÉ

Without
Music

**REFINERS
PUBLISHERS**
+233(0)556998317
refinerspublishers@yahoo.com

Acknowledgement

A sincere acknowledgment to my mother who has been my strength and stay all these years, my grandmother whose boundless love continues to steep and my step father who has been a creative muse. This book wouldn't have been possible without you.

Content

Author's Moments

The poems are the author's moments and personal recollections of grief and a journey to exhilaration. With over 70 original poems, Without Music is divided into five categories, with themes ranging from healing, pain, religion, loss and love that will inspire you greatly.

Letters

I Wish I Could

I wish to tell you,
Oh good friend of mine,
About the years and years of nurtured pain,
And tears and tears that failed to dry,
I wish I had words,
Befitting words to describe a moaning heart,
How I wish, good friend of mine,
How I wish that I could.

To Sister

Hello sister!
If you are there,
How was the day?

My side here,
Burns of sun like coal,
The deep hurt with pleasure,
Blows my mind,
It makes it clear,
Life isn't ending today.

Hello sister!
If you are there,
Then I'd like you to know,
We are all fine like gold,
Dazzling and sparkling,
And this makes it clear,
Life is simply better with you in mind.

Coming Along

The cloud hangs dreadfully,
Often dark with no glow of sun beam,
Looks like that of yesterday,
When I covered in the tempest,
And feared the shooting rage,
With mild wild thunderbolt,
So I am happy you are coming along.

My barren luck has not gone far,
And my disappointments strike resemblance,
They are similar to ones long days of search,
A search for soothe in others,
For perfection if it still exists,
Only to find they have not much purpose.

Coming Along

But the happy days,
They were like when I took a pen,
And drafted young resilient words,
In such days my mind would think of olives and roses.

I've packed into one box,
My insane journey of a thousand years,
I will drag it down bottom of my chest,
There is nothing to miss so long as,
You my brother are coming along.

My Papa

Oh Papa!
Why drift to the other side?
At such young my age,
Why leave us here to remain in yesterday?

Oh my irreplaceable Papa!
The sun rising with no You,
Is as though a starless night,
So why drift farther?
Why leave us here in dangerous despair?
Why let my quest remain?

Oh my dear Papa!
Why not open the door?
Touch to see if it won't break,
Death is just a mile away.

My Papa

I'm fumbling in this state,
Where my heart wants to melt,
So try to touch, see if it won't break,
So I will be able to touch your face,
And keep close with your eyes.

Oh my irreplaceable one!
Do you see the hole I have become?
This thick between your world and mine,
Is as faint as a glass partition,
On which I lean tight.

It is a mere mirage,
Through which I envision a date,
The frail bridge between your world and mine,
Is not too faint for my hope,

My Papa

Or too fat for my love,
All that matters is your breath,
So one more time,
Take that deep breath.

Agu

Thank you for writing it my friend,

What you have is unshaken strength,

Despite what the war stole from you,

Though it left you broken ribs with a fragile wrist,

You didn't shy away like the jillion others,

I envy your invested time,

And the heavy words you bear,

Thank you for the dawns you endured ghost-haunts,

And for withstanding the era,

For because you felt pain without a cause,

Your life is worth honouring,

So Agu many thanks,

Thank you for smelling the scent of plain sheets,

And for quenching our thirst.

Lost Moments

Isn't it obvious we lost the moment?
Time is such a short sense,
Fragile is each moment that it is short-lived.
I'm recalling the passing of each lost moment,
Where we failed to make memories,
I guess we lost it all.

I love to imagine us at the ball,
Where you wear black suit and I tighten your tie
you are perfect.
I am in red silk gown with black shoes you bought,
And when I fake that I know your favourite colour,
Then it must be green.

We are driving up the hill,
Between the mountains we swing,

Lost Moments

And you teach me to skate,
So I know your voice as smooth as the wind.

In a flash of this holy fantasy,
We sail on a boat,
Saddling back and forth,
Then I think of us on our last date,
Where we laugh at pathetic songs,
And these memories I may never have forgotten,
Yet it is sad we lost the moment,
Like a ray no one noticed.

Deranged

Did I tell you my love?
Of this fierce vertigo,
About what love is doing to me?
And though you may not understand baby,
I really see lights;
Great sparks and arcs of light,
And crystal chandeliers,
Though there are none.

Did I tell you my lord?
That you cause my rage?
And you make me deranged?
This your love pushes me back and forth,
And I am on the brick,
The very last brick.

But didn't I tell you babe?
Of my obedience and devotion?

Deranged

That I hear your voice shutting me out,
Even when you aren't there,
And suddenly I want to be a stone!
You make me wanna be a stone.
So that while I'm breaking and cracking,
Even then I'll be hard and unbending for you.

Hello from a Neighbour

Hello there,

It's me,

That your old neighbour,

From across the street,

Behind the kiosk,

If you have a moment,

Then do spare me a second.

I was wondering,

If you could at least try,

Try to be nice,

To care,

To help,

Try to appreciate,

And try not to resent me so much.

If you can,

Then pleading, I urge you,

Letters 19

Hello from a Neighbour

To try something sane,
There is no need for gossip,
Do not step on my toes,
Do not judge me,
Try to be concerned,
If you had at least tried,
Then you would know,
That life is tiresome,
And our fights are excess baggage.

If we try other things aside the usual,
Then you'll know I have been;
Not only your neighbour but a friend,
A caretaker and sister,
And I could wish you well,
That all I am, like you,
Is one generous but troubled woman.

Introvert

Did you ask if I am an introvert?
You wouldn't know how safe I am inside,
My mind is a weaved forest,
And I'm in a wide cobweb,
The direction of the passing breeze,
Is an act of detoxification,
Yet truly my lights suddenly went off,
The sound of laughter at bay,
And I am briskly going down this tunnel,
Fighting hard so as to not get damp,
I'm aching because you've,
Just mocked me an introvert.

Imaginarily

Imaginarily,
I just packed my bags and called a cap,
Imaginarily,
I'm walking down the stairs; I just left you a note,
Imaginarily,
You're one big jerk,
A dream waiting to come true,
But you've only found out now,
Imaginarily,
I just walked out your door,
Driving along the road,
Imaginarily,
You've just realized that you've lost,
And I've won the battle within,
But sadly and practically,
I've just stepped at the door,
With the grocery bag in hand,
Still hanging around waiting for a change.

Magic

My Indifference

It is already dawn,
Down here and up there,
Neither is the rise of the sun,
Nor the trail of the moon,
At this place where I lay.

Grandma in Mind

Had I not met grandma,
Then maybe I would be the worst fool,
She was warm as flesh,
But maybe I wouldn't believe when told,
That she was as a real saint,
Had I not met grandma,
Who smelt of lily fragrance,
And would sleep in sand so I lie on mat,
Then maybe life would be unfortunate,
Grandma had grey hair and pale skin,
But her eyes were always,
That of a gracious mother.

Young Suitor

Marry me,
My young suitor with the books,
Line a parlour for me,
Make me your guest at the parquet,
And let us dance a dance of royals,
Like a fancy English woman,
I shall wear pompous gown,
And we'll hold hands,
While my head drums for a noble man.

My young suitor from the shelves,
You that flip through archives and treasury,
You will marry me, won't you?
The author of five and more,
I heard of 'Jude's and May's'
So I heard,
That you are the author of six and more,
'Many a Day, Life Goes Around',

Young Suitor

And 'Mild Will, Calling Home',
If for a while you think,
That you found true company in me,
Then I wouldn't mind to,
Gift you a rocking chair and a pen.

Sinking Sun

There is nothing as radiant,
As compared to a yellow sinking sun,
No, not the scorching sun,
I am admiring the one that is simply tired,
It has such divinity,
I see it waving goodbye,
Then I see it sinking,
Into an empty foamy cloud.

.

When We Grow Old

On Thursday when we grow old,
And become granny and grandpa we longed to be,
You'll smoke pipe and chew cola,
You'll forgo beer and take pills,
Use the walker and leave the car,
You'll talk less sense,
And let the children waver,
On Thursday when we finally grow old,
Your worries will turn wrinkles,
While you battle to restore health,
Besides, these are all we live for.

.

Sincerity

I am sincerely wearing the gown,
From top to my feet,
And my nerves so high,
My collarbone out with no chains in gold,
I'm in a lace that's sparking royally,
From side to side but what is vital,
Is I'm sincerely wearing my gown.

.

Exterior Decor

That you don't see the goodness,

Doesn't mean it isn't there,

Life has bountiful of choices,

So choose to see life,

As though it were a quick moment of sadness,

Then death ,

Like a small extension of that moment,

See life,

Like a flash of beautiful crystal light,

Then death,

Like a flash of blurred dim light,

See life,

Only when it just gotten better,

Then death,

Like you've just lost sense of that style,

Exterior Decor

See life,
As if it's goodwill and self love that matter,
Then death,
As though it isn't your loss.

.

The Oil

Knowledge for the human,
Ought to be the greatest,
And the lamp in us need the oil to lit,
Yet only this oil of education,
Shall set you into a spark,
Or even a burning flame.

.

Cancer

It was yesterday at twenty,
There it all began;
You were forlornly subjected and had this curse,
And you were lost when it all emerged,
But then, you were at twenty so you took the blame.

In those foretimes,
You were dark and shredding,
The feeling was plain,
And you were about to be slain,
That hearts were beating for you.

At twenty you did fail,
That was you crawling;
The cold ending of a lion,
But despite the fall at twenty,
You ate fat, you drunk eggs,
You broke jugs, you cracked bones,

Cancer

While the doctors whispered and tried your blood.

At twenty you spat the broth,
Because you were truly in pain,
Yet you had dried eyes and will,
And harnessed it though the taste was gall,
But you couldn't have cried,
At twenty, sorrow wasn't a thing,
Even today, six feet underground it still isn't,
Truth wasn't a thing but joy was everything,
You paid your depth,
So it ended right there, at twenty.

The Wind

I turned my side at night,
And whilst I lay,
I heard the wilful sound,
Or was it banging?
I was paying heed as it wiped the sand,
Then I knew it was no other than the wind,
The wind that welcomed the rain.

Light in the Tunnel

The light sleeping in you,
Has the ability to bright,
And lighten any hole that you find yourself,
But only by realizing you are in that hole,
Where others need your light,
Do you actually shine.

Owl in the Dark

I wrote deep into the night,
And my eyes began scrolling their way in my head,
My finger clenched and my mind froze,
Yet I am still an owl in the dark night,
So much I never give up.

Miracles

God's favours are everywhere;
On the day of our birth,
And on the day of our death,
Our first words and our last breath,
It's that miracle leading us,
To everywhere and everyday,
Parts are the friends who give their all,
And relatives who are not always there but true,
The strangers we meet;
Who unconditionally give their love,
And believe in us for as long as we live.

The miracles, my friend,
Are all over in the air;
In the arc of colours that grace the sky,
In you and in me.

Miracles

If you look closely,
Then you will see each day is a priceless gift,
That you may choose to see otherwise,
But when you see it the way it is,
Life begins to make sense,
The struggles become worthy,
Forgiveness becomes a need,
So does each broken piece falls in place.

Light Sleep

My body is overcome with cold,
All round my aging eyes,
And I'm done putting a fight with my bed,
I'm sleeping again and again,
I've left tonight far away.

Sound

Some years ago you had,
Wished for a night like this,
Only one night like this,
Where there is a shoulder to cry on,
Where you'll have someone listen,
But when you failed,
You grew touch though tender,
Strong though frail,
You pulled yourself together,
And then you wore your very best.

Sculpt

I stood at the mountain,
And imagined a fall,
Holding the scarf high,
And I felt beautiful,
I pictured myself,
A flawless princess.

Mute

I close my eye and image beauty,
That life is idyll,
And that life is sweet,
In my mind's eye,
All I could dream of this vast world,
Is true happiness and mirth,
And of calm souls as a river,
I also wish for serenity,
And no more carcass for us;
We the unschooled and unskilled.

No Competition at All

I don't care what bothers the world,
What becomes of Africa,
What is trending in America,
Or the typhoons and quakes in Asia,
Neither do I sleep less,
Because of the reigning,
Kings and queens in Europe,
Nor care about what plagues the world,
Of its immigrants and migrants,
Because I am sure to die,
Die in Africa and leave America,
Forget Europe and if possible,
Experience the rebirth in Asia.

Alteration

Love from a Black Man

I am on ma knees asking God why?
Why you strong and bold?
But me meek and weak?
Oh Lord!
What's beauty in the voice?
Your mouth is sore and chilling,
And the void in ma heart matters little,
Why? I am woman,
Feminine, that can't say Stop or No,
You hit me and I scream,
Then you say SHUSH!
Your love at its best,
This must be true love from a black man.

You've groomed me,
Oh baby I am cooked!
Into something, something,

Love from a Black Man

Something like one unfailing green-eyed woman,
Though I know you licking her clit,
And smooching her lips,
Baby I am so Shushed.

'All men are the same, it is not in them'
So I believe you do loove me,
Despite the women and adultery,
You still loove me,
I tell ya this must be true love from a black man,
You don't say it but you show,
My black eye says,
This must be true love from a black man.

In the sight of this shitty pain,
I still make your bath and soup,
Then you remember me;
The Me you left behind,

Love from a Black Man

You touch me quickly,
Entering and Cuming as though our last,
'They don't show affection, it is not in them'
And that is how it is,
True love from a black man.

When a Man Fails

The pain you feel when you hit your toes,
Hard against a rock,
Is the kind a man feels when he fails,
You look at your bleeding toe,
Then look at the unbowed stone,
Yet there is absolutely nothing you can do.

My Mother Nags

My mother nags,
As though she were,
Of the last black race of beings alive,
Like she had fasted in the last plague,
And had survived a world war,
Or smeared dust as clay,
She nags,
As though she were,
Born in mid eighties and lost a twin,
Like her father baptized her with ashes,
And she had lived voiceless,
Under a dead branch,
My mother nags,
As though there is no tomorrow,
As though we have no gods of our own,
Perhaps had she been barren?
Perhaps had she not a bed?

My Mother Nags

My mother nags,
As though she never stayed on the third floor,
She screeches like a flat tyre,
Chirps like an angry bird,
Like others have no baggage,
Yet it's just us, she and I.

Greed

We may stop living,
But it's only a misconception,
And even our jumpy heart,
May result from greed,
The unnecessary moments of action,
And vengeance uncalled for,
Few regrets out of our own cowardice,
That we butcher one another.

The Peak

Each height is at its peak,
That I feel dizzy while I gaze,
Not much of confidence I have,
Rather the hope of a last stare,
But for you to help in my climbing,
You give me a ladder,
After you break off the steps,
So how do I reach the apex?

The Beauty in Death

There is beauty in death;
It is exquisite and radiant,
Aunty saw it too, that was on Friday;
When it came like snow,
The mute resilient beauty,
It had that lemon fragrance at the gate,
And it spoke English to anyone,
It wasn't exactly as expected of the cold word,
But it was everything as the wind blowing,
It was the sun slowly hissing,
And it was the droplets of rain,
So sometimes aunty saw it like frost,
But other times she saw it like a woman;
Any mother who had bows behind and blades in hand,
But on Friday, death was a man:
It had beard, it had a neck, it had a chest,
Death was her bitter husband.

Alteration 55

Caged

I am that bird you hid,
In a tube you covered well,
You suffocate me and I am dizzy,
Unable to fly so I will die,
I will die young and flyable.

A Journey of No Return

I won't return,
Even when the rain beats me,
I won't return,
Even when I'm burnt by the sun,
I will go miles and miles far away,
A journey of no return.

With my last breath and guts,
I journeyed with strength,
Moving further each day,
Even my footmarks I wiped away,
That there was no sight of me.

Here we are today,
No more me and no more you,
Now there is no more us,
No more yelling,
No more fighting,

Alteration 57

A Journey of No Return

And no more emotions I can hardly express.

Not a bit of you I miss,
It was rugged but I carried none of you,
Here, I am pulled down like a wall,
And torn down by this merciless rain and cruel sun,
But this journey I will not return.

I have grown a thick skin,
I have gotten rough and round then bold,
And I have grown arrogant, fierce then careless,
Today, I can actually hurt you,
And look the other way,
I am now twice that one you knew.

The Monster

I have come to terms,
Terms with that one monster,
A symbol of my unfortunate fate,
The monster who reminds me,
That I am a beggar,
A beggar with no choice.

That monster,
A mirror reflecting this broken heart of mine,
A monster,
Who tells me I'm a tree with no root,
A monster who is at his best,
As long as I don't have a voice,
As long as I don't have a choice,
A monster who came in,
Invited and called upon,
By the very thing I treasure.

Surprises

Those creepy things;
Science molecules in mummy's tummy,
They must have heard,
Of how people turned,
From embryos to giants,
Of how each man walked free and eased freely,
Indeed life actually isn't that awful,
Sometimes there are things we laugh about,
Though most times there are things to cry for,
The more we live the more we hear nerve wracking news,
We see more of certain things,
Things strong enough to drive us mad.

My Brother

This side my brother,
Isn't what you think,
It wasn't what we hoped,
But this side my brother,
Is what we have,
All that we have,
Is this side my brother.

Your Attitude

I know that attitude,
This attitude;
The attitude where you have all,
Yet you want more,
I had that attitude,
This attitude;
That I had all and wanted more,
But in this cloudburst,
Under the scorching sun,
For God's sake,
I have given up all of it,
All of that attitude,
This attitude,
The attitude where you have all but want more,
That now I have barely more,
But forsaken the unnecessary.

Like Me

No one is exactly like you,

But you and I,

We do have a lot in common,

There are times we want to give up,

Yet we don't have the courage,

We are simply a saphead the world mistakes for a genius,

We tell ourselves that we are tired,

Wishing to roll into thin invisible balls,

Yet we cannot,

A part of the similarity is we aren't sure what the future holds,

Just like me you are uncertain that you can move on,

But when you wake to meet a new day,

You just hiss and walk through,

Everything seems lame,

Just like me you wear a smile,

And you want to impress,

But you think of fear and you fumble,

Like Me

Like me you want a sign; A miracle or likely,
You don't want anyone telling you about what the Lord said,
Now you want a one on one talk with Him,
Just like me,
You will like to fall,
And die right there,
In the middle of that difficulty,
And on that day death will be saving your life,
Like the millions of by-passers,
You do cry,
But only in an empty room,
The other side of brave.

Our Greatest Enemies

Our greatest enemies,
Are not at the office or at home,
Our enemies may be out,
On the street and in cluster of people,
But the greatest enemies of all,
Remain our own addictions,
They are those things inside us;
Our vibrant fears,
Those actions and inactions unaccounted for,
Our greatest enemies will always be,
Our overriding ambitions,
The aging ago, and judgements,
Our greatest enemies are;
Our moments of indecisions,
Our possessive desires,
Our greatest enemy of all time,
Is when we tame the mind,

Our Greatest Enemies

To series of obstructions,
And are indifference to pains and aches,
Our greatest enemies are our own wings,
Those that make us too heavy to fly,
Our greatest enemies are not from outside,
But rather within us.

A Drunkard's Legacy

He beats his chest,
From the square everyone watches,
Only the pots of liquor are his,
His wife left him for this,
For a coward man,
His daughters have become atonements,
Children of a troubled man,
They too are home idle,
With flies hovering over their heads,
Very soon his creditors will come,
Asking for their dues and he will find excuse,
Even the lifeless thatches have come to a halt,
They wait for the set date,
Only to strike and fall ablaze.

The Character

You are perfect for the cameras,
You are right for the lines,
Gorgeous and bold,
You have tactics but you're slow,
Like a sweet French wine,
You're perfect for the lens.

You've been a pro and a champ,
Who will always be on screen,
And right for each role bestowed,
The plays are great and so is the orchestra.

You sound so well but you're not,
You are perfectly imperfect for life,
Away from these lights,
Without the punch-lines,
You're a bad habit;
Neither sincere nor a champ,
You have always not played so well in life.

Alteration 68

Last Liquor

I stood by the last liquor,
And went out to greet folks,
By the last liquor,
Came shame and inverted grace,
By the last liquor,
Each soul went out the door,
And dad threw out his faith,
He drenched our white gowns,
By the last liquor,
I bet he was swinging;
Inside an imagined swing,
And there he was,
Till night left,
By this very liquor,
Mary went away,
She would be dammed if she stayed.

Things Apart

The world itself induces frustration,
I learnt there is this thing to check my eyes,
And another to check the arm,
I learnt this thing could check my heart,
And another could check my blood,
And there have always been,
Something to check something,
Like the thermometer for my pressure,
Or a thing like scale for my weight,
So I might be checking it all,
Now that I am depressed,
And my heart races like a marathon,
Because now I see everything,
Everything wrong when I stare,
At those same roses through the window,
And though I've turned,
From funerals and closed my eyes,
My ears constantly hear of its tantrum.

Road Side

Allow me sick,
Leave me and let me die,
There is no more to live for,
Yet a lot to die for,
But if there is someone in mind,
Then it's the man at the sea,
The women by the well,
The daughters feeding hungry birds,
And those sons beating rice,
While I await my God,
Allow me some pleasure in grains and sex,
Because if there is something else I can afford,
Then it's perhaps death,
Death and only death.

Growing Out Age

Seventeen days away,
Growing feels the same,
Same wondering and failures,
But it could be fair,
If it didn't tatter my heart,
Shiver my strength,
Or trigger fear and distress,
Growing seem a necessity,
But I'm lost in thoughts,
And in the world of responsibilities and barriers,
That will be eventual boundaries.

Growing is heavenly but a waste,
Because in the end,
I am still that child;
Who washed and broke plates,
Took errands in exchange for coins,
And in sixty years to come,

Alteration 72

Growing Out Age

I will remain a child,
One who didn't drink at night,
But fell frequently and sprained a leg.

The Church's Sin

Brethren in the Lord, is it only me?
Who sees the church as lost,
There are no saints, and it all seeks fortune.

If it is only me that sees no value,
And bewildered at the ultimate pledge,
Of no souls but riches won,
Such that I see its venom,
Then brethren in the Lord,
You must be blind and ignorant of truth,
The truth is, change knows no comfort.

For you poor brethren,
You're wholly convicted,
During preaching or deliverance,
And amid religion and science,
But rich brethren,
You're vital and functional,
And only your kind is born of the Lord.

Alteration 74

Beat Him Slowly

There is something we should have done,
When Ewreku raped Masa,
And got his fair skin burnt,
It was hard watching it,
But not as painful as living it.

When Ewreku robbed the chain store,
And got his blood smeared on the wall,
It felt weird but not right,
And I thought of;
The weight of the sin,
The innocence of the punisher,
And the atonement scene.
I called him twice,
Yet only echoes yielded response,
And I knew we should have,
Beat him slowly,
Let him live small,

Beat Him Slowly

Before he died through it all,
Besides what bliss is in destruction?

The Split

Yesterday's rain was a misfortune,
One sad storm that swept clean our home,
And left behind dust that ruined our garment.

Its courage crumbled the old tree,
That no one could think of,
So we wake up today,
From dreams into sorrows,
Knowing harm has been done.

We hear dirges,
Dirges that are on the way,
And we feel the tears,
Finding ways down our cheeks,
That even Araba's unborn child,
Understands the mourner carrying her,
But we also find warmth,
And comfort in black clothes.

Alteration 77

The Split

The weeping sky appears dubious,
Because with grandpa gone,
We detangle our unity,
And make fuse over his leftovers.

I Cannot Breathe

Camouflage

The air is getting cold,
I can see thick fogs meeting,
Up with the sky half and half,
And the clouds moulding,
Into trees and carriages,
I can hear bells ringing,
Christmas sounding so new,
Children singing melodies at dawn,
And red and white coats clustering.

Yet there are no carols, no real wheels,
Truth is, no true flies,
And no magic to stain the sky,
The harmattan is coming,
Though apples arrived earlier,
It was more convenient to see,
The land dry and gushing.

Camouflage

I know Christmas is about trees,
I see Christmas is about fake trees,
Rubber roots, bogus fruits and leaves,
But for some reason,
I guess we still hear the deaf,
But I want to know,
Why do we feed the girls?
Why we give the beggar,
Why only now orphans are sacred?
For the past eleven, where have we been?

End of the World

It was one of those fine days,
The dull and drooping sky didn't come ,
With extreme burning of the sun,
But it was one of those mundane days,
So we all went about,
From one friend to another,
We all went about.

It started to rain,
It went from little drops to huge drops,
And began filling every pothole,
Then started to flow,
But it had only began,
And didn't promise to end well,
It was as though the nearest sea,
Had overflown into our home,
Then crumble the doors into our rooms,
Even today I can firmly recall,
How my neighbours used china bowl to fetch them out.

End of the World

There was nowhere to go,
And no place to hide,
But it was the flood we knew,
Rolling its mighty self and showing off,
Then in a minute everything burnt,
From where the fire?
That we didn't know,
But it was fire on water.

When I recall of Noah's ark,
And Sodom and Gomorrah,
Then it had to be,
The end of the world,
Where everyone burnt,
Our children died,
And our husbands drowned,
But after all had ended,
It was I and my neighbour that perished.

We Failed Him

Why are we so wretched?
The end normally pitiful,
It's all thanks to our wrinkled skin,
That once was pale as smooth,
And won the hearts of men.

It was truly grandpa by the road,
Whom the sun made blind,
His feet swollen,
And his skin coiled like autumn leaves,
Like a conscious madman,
Grandpa slept on the street,
Where bright days were a curse,
And the rains to him a spear.

The Senses

What my heart is feeling,
My eyes may not see,
And exactly what my ears may hear,
So also my heart may not know,
Because they are fatly unique;
My heart to love and injustice,
My ears to contamination and rage,
And my eyes to lust and belittlement,
These senses however, they choose to play the game,
Each to his strength and passion.

The Taxpayer

What is there to tell?
That the taxpayer is,
Paying duff Eagles,
Or that these Eagles,
Are unapologetic looters,
These things give me migraine,
And my head is spinning,
But what else to do?
Except to buy them saloons,
While I hasten for rickety bus.

Then again who does it best?
Who votes and waits counting?
Who takes loan and pays interest?
Who farms and trades in drought?
Who sings anthems of hope?
And who pays this country's debt?

The Taxpayer

But to think I face the worst;
Line for health insurance,
Queue at maternity ward,
And commend the wretched system.

I feel programmed and molested,
That while flowers lay in vase,
I sleep below the bridge,
And I dunno who else to tell,
That this tax payer is sick,
And in a state of pyromania.

Nothing I Do

This country gets scarier by the sec,
And pricy every hour,
The government has failed me;
As a citizen, as a woman and as human,
Perhaps why I'd rather,
Not battle with the papers,
Because all is soon to hit up.

Because medicine has grown,
As expensive as refined gold,
So these days when I walk,
I feel the stares at my back,
As though they chase me,
For all that I don't have,
And the children sorely,
Pulling my dress for coins,
They have become poorer,
Something you see through,

Nothing I Do

Their peculiar creasy muddy feet,
And later with the preacher,
Who conspires for my last penny,
And promises of miracles unseen,
Or the invisible wealth I suppose is in Christ,
But this rottenness makes it hard,
Because of the many I endure,
Is the despair of street hawkers,
Who will sell me anything,
From flour to aphrodisiac,
So I suppose in a way,
I may use some magic,
While thinking through this madness.

Home

With the way this country moves,
The youth and theft,
Of the gutters and flood,
Traffic jams and road,
Workers and strike,
Road accidents and cars,
And to top it all is,
The politicians and talk,
Now I have decided,
To quit my job and sleep home,
Where I will face either one of the two,
The second coming of Christ,
Or my untimely death.

Peace

Why such psych?
Wishing for sound,
Yet seek by those at war,
Hear this good heart please!
So the peace desired,
Prevails either rain or shine,
And so we can shy away,
From all that's destructive,
And loss in this election.

Why the Government

One of these days,
I will talk with the government,
And ask, what's the need for votes?
When all left is secluded bones,
Ask why the need for limo,
Can't Kantanka be improved?
One of these days,
The people will wake up from slumber,
And ask the government why?
Ask where about the loans?
When our lives have seen no change!
Ask why the urge to go abroad,
When our country still lies in your debt,
Did you learn just theory?
Now see you can't create at all?
One of these days,
I will ask the government why?

Why the Government

Did they leave the knowledge abroad?
You came back with just the shreds?
One day the plebs will wipe blindness,
And ask the government, why?

Why the need to study law?
How about the farms?
Ask why the lip-service,
Can't you for once be true?
Why the need to improve modernity?
When the locals need the chance,
Why, you still import fancy chairs?
When all we need is some aid,
One of these days,
Even children will see the light,
Then ask the government why?

Why the Government

Why, we can't afford tuition?
Yet you exchange cedis for dollar,
And is it that your office is genetic?
Only relative resume when you vacate,
One day the youth will wake up from slumber,
Then ask corrupt officials why?

Is it that your pay isn't enough?
Even we manage our pennies,
You've turned education to some system,
Full of depravity and stress,
So what's the use of your degrees?
That you are masters in some field?
You learnt our problems and solutions,
Yet beneficiaries so you won't help,
One of these days,
I will talk with the government,
Then ask the old men, why?

Revolution

After today's reconciliation,
I will make efforts to remember,
The previous days of war,
But there will be no need,
No need for the old indoors,
Or for school children on street,
And the need to hold flags high,
While chanting tsoboi!
And I wouldn't have to ask,
What country am I?
But Kofi is gone and Ama is lost,
You know how much our youth love freedom,
So you may hear of countless sacrifices,
And of the idiots called elites,
Or how in mourning the huge loss,
They could only build the state necropolis,
Not for each other but for them,
So it becomes our income generation project;

Revolution

Where Ama's name is curved,
Curved out of the walls by the artist,
Such that people pay for photographs,
And leave with the laughs.

Solidarity

Tell me the needs of the people,
And I'll go sleepless,
Just to find you solutions,
Because I am the people,
Of them and governance,
And though I'm into no politics,
Because it is temporal survival,
I am still leaning on the solidarity of the people.

Muse

My God

Did I tell you about my God?
He I have been serving,
For 200 years in the farms,
Did I tell you about God?
In white skin and robes,
A symbol of holiness,
Yet led me astray.

Did I tell you about my Lord?
Who watched me plead and bleed,
Bleeding from master's strokes,
Yet from each whip I endured,
For my Lord gave me strength.

Did I tell you about my Lord?
Who watched my innocent babies,
Grow into men and women slaves,

My God

Oh I tell you that he watched!
From sun-up to sun-down,
And across the vase fields,
He watched!
Then I would wonder,
That is there no God?
Each time there was a kill,
Is there really no God?
In brown skin and kinky hair,
Is there no God at all?

Minutes to Racism

It's the dawn of ice age,
And disheartening as this is,
It's few minutes to racism,
And there is complete incapacitation,
Transgression and discrimination!
Then partly of damnation,
Condemnation and ignominy!
But before the unfailing inequality,
Let me pack my bags and head away,
Let me wipe my tears,
While I empty my closet,
For we are at the dawn of ice age,
And before the hatred leads me astray,
Let me quickly catch the next bus.

Do You Know?

The children at the bosom,
May I know if you know?
That in some part of this world,
You appear less significant,
And the least privileged,
Because If we were playing with colours,
Then you'll be black and less sophisticated,
You'll be degraded and yes!
You'll suffer from grave stare,
Because your colour cowardly,
Is fundamental for judgement,
That's why I care to know,
If the children already understand,
Both race and the class.

Tender Strength

We walked through thorns,
And when we reached a crossroad,
Mother carried the wood,
Which I had bundled,
And my sister tied,
During those times,
We showed strength,
Because the weather was soon to change,
For us to return slaves.

Talking Drum

I turned and tossed,
My body in a swing,
That the drum in my chest beats,
That if such a day might fall,
That I become one piece of art,
A talking drum if I am not,
Then a dancing swing I shall remain.

Strong

Hold it up!
Strong in the soil,
Uproot it not,
And don't let go,
Till it flies high,
Too high to be caught up with.

The Ray

Today I shall be the ray,
As the sun delay,
My doctrines I shall,
Teach other comrades,
Then walk away.

The Day's Empire

It's in lightening and candles,
The independence of our nation,
Called the efforts of untold history,
Standing firm to make,
One fine news today.

An Eagle's Plight

I am here wondering,
If the talk about Africa is over,
And I know I'm hovering,
Hovering over what has been lost;
The decays and remains of the race,
The branches are no longer strong,
All strength has been lost,
To either fire or thirsty earth,
So I will fly miles away,
And lay down my worries.

The Way We Walk the Walk

With the strong men in front,
We women behind,
Our children at our backs,
And the yielding sun keeping the watch,
We aren't sure of the journey,
How far or short more,
But our instinct living.

We close our eyes from the merciless sun,
But with carefree mind,
We left the bodies of our fellows;
That of weak men and women,
Whose corpse we couldn't carry.
The footprints we leave behind,
Are not necessarily intentional,
But when I turn,
I do not see them clean,
That alone increases my hope,

The Way We Walk the Walk

That if we never get there,
We could someday be favoured,
With good burials at home.

Before the Sun Sets

Just before the sun sets,
Let's not forget sorrowful days,
Days of darkness and plaque,
When we had said,
That we will stick together,
So before the sun sets,
Let me make my stand clear,
That right here where I stand,
Is where I will be,
Waiting for the sun ray.

Peace Keeping

How can Akpa stir the war?
Yet say it is rescuing,
Saving us from blood-shed,
While he plots the murder,
Of our hand-some children,
So I dare to say,
It is joy to die in mother's arm,
She will cry and carry you home,
But for that red-haired stranger;
Akpa will kick you with his boot,
Then spread the word of your loss.

Dreams of Freedom

I have yearned long,
In every instance for freedom,
Heard of you once,
That you're playing hard to get,
Like that gorgeous dame,
Who knows her worth,
If you are sweet as her,
Then I know I truly want you.

With society being a daily prison,
Only few listen to inmate's wisdom,
We all are;
Not just physically incarcerated,
But our minds as well as the soul,
Both mind and soul are encaged,
But we keep on the go,
One cell to the other.

Dreams of Freedom

Until the day humanity fades,
We will lock in a box,
Taking a forever rest,
But I do;
Want to break free a bird,
Free my mind, body and soul,
Help me make the world better,
Challenge stereotype if it isn't obvious,
So that when my body fades,
My spirit wouldn't,
Because when the time comes,
I am helpless and immured.

Songs of Africa

We still mourn for the rest,
And yearn for the past,
For those stolen by the thief,
And the lands they left insecure,
But when the old take a seat,
The young must pay homage,
Saying they rode behind,
Our ignorance and pride,
But tell grandpa it is enough,
Rather face today's misery,
And give way for growth,
For development and justice,
A lineage to brag of,
And grow grains with grace.

Errands for Aid

I went behind your kitchen,
Hiding between your pots,
And then I saw your kitten,
I also met the rat,
During those nights I turned it my place,
But you know me well,
I'm lingering here for errands.

You give me what you have,
And mine is thank you,
And though I'm begging,
I am not always a beggar,
You know me well,
So pray my people never unite,
Look in the sky and make a wish,
Wish that sanity never returns,
Say here is better than there,
So when I ask give me more,

Errands for Aid

Because we are scavengers,
There is neither food nor water,
No shelter to lay my head,
So I am a willing pauper.

If we unite today,
I shall leave your kitchen,
And start my journey,
You know me well,
That of wisdom we are made,
Good at everything we remain,
The solid found of your wealth,
With unity that seizes exploitation,
We will mount a wall and that is when you fall.

About the Author

Winnie Akousika DOGBÉ was born to Ghanaian and Togolese parents, she holds a B.A in Communication Studies from the Ghana Institute of Journalism. Akousika is a corporate writer and a PR person. She is currently working on her children's novel and a collection of short stories.